BOB CHILCOTT

SUN DANCE

from *Organ Dances*

MUSIC DEPARTMENT

UNIVERSITY PRESS

Sun Dance

(from Organ Dances, for organ and orchestra)

BOB CHILCOTT
(b. 1955)

I Chorus coupled to Ped.
II Chorus coupled to I
III Solo reed

This piece is a slightly modified version of the fifth movement from *Organ Dances*, for organ solo, strings and percussion.

Printed in Great Britain

OXFORD UNIVERSITY PRESS, MUSIC DEPARTMENT, GREAT CLARENDON STREET, OXFORD OX2 6DP

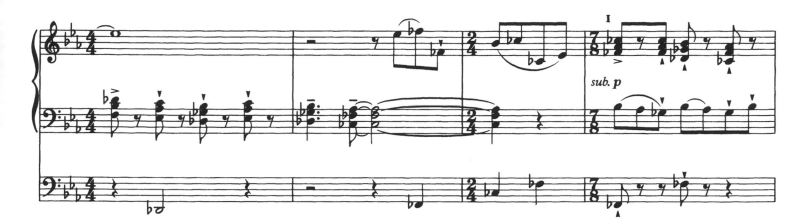

Un poco meno mosso

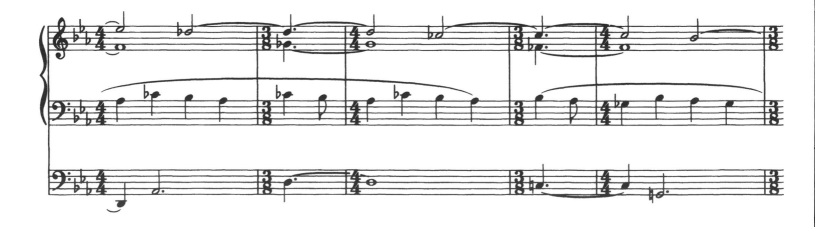

Tempo primo

marcato

Solo (III)

f

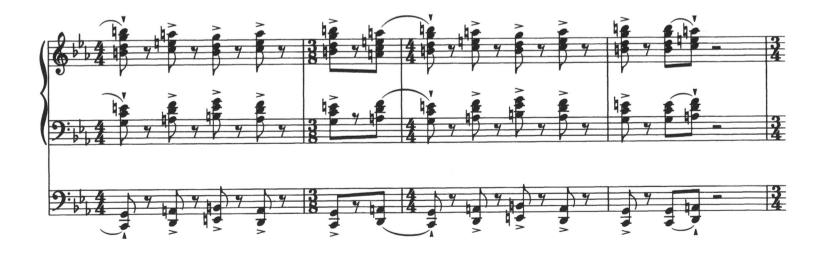

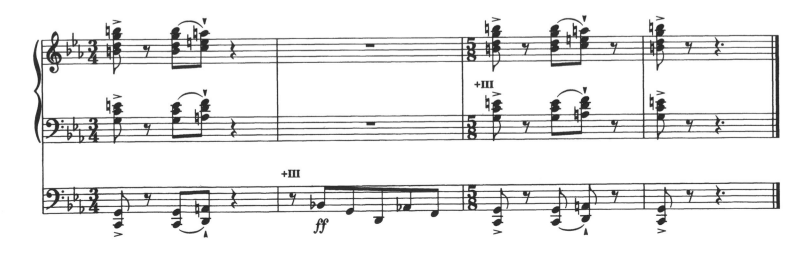